Moments

WITH

Birds

ALVIN MAST

Moments

WITH

Birds

ALVIN MAST

ISBN: 978-1-63813-008-6

All photographs in this book were taken by the author.

Cover and text layout design: Kristi Yoder

Printed in China

Published by:
TGS International
P.O. Box 355
Berlin, Ohio 44610 USA
Phone: 330.893.4828
Fax: 330.893.2305
www.tgsinternational.com

Cover photo: This stunning Great Egret posed for the author near Venice, Florida.

Dedication

This book is dedicated to my wife Esther, who is my lifetime friend and best birding partner. She puts me to shame at finding birds. But I don't mind since she always tells me where they are.

   I also dedicate it to my daughter Rachel, who, adorned with binoculars and a kindred spirit, often goes with us to field and forest. I'm grateful to her for giving me tips on writing and for doing the preliminary editing for this work.

A Palm Warbler provides a memorable moment for the author.

Table of Contents

Introduction

"The flowers appear on the earth; the time of the singing of birds is come, and the voice of the turtle is heard in our land" (Song of Solomon 2:12).

Birds are one of the greatest wonders of God's creation. They can be found almost anywhere—from the oceans to the highest mountains. They round out the world like candles on a cake, living in desert and jungle. Many birds migrate thousands of miles with no map or help from anyone. They travel freely from one country to the next; world leaders cannot impose their laws on them. They are our friends and worthy of our attention.

The world is loud and demanding and is screaming for our time and attention. For the sake of sanity and physical health, we must have some quiet time once in a while. One way of experiencing that quiet time is to go to the fields and woods. Watching the birds and listening to their songs is something I never tire of. Many a time over the years it has helped me get the kinks of stress out of my life.

I am an amateur photographer and spend hours outdoors observing nature and taking pictures of birds. My friend and birding partner Duane Nisly from Costa Rica says it well, "You really haven't seen a bird until you have a good picture of it."

Some of my best birding experiences have been in Costa Rica. I don't think I will ever forget the birding trip with my friend Mark. It was dark when we pulled into the place where we were going to stay in the highlands. It was also very cold.

The cabins were studs and boards. A feeble attempt was made to warm my cabin with a tiny electric heater, but it had little effect. I shivered as I climbed, fully dressed, under the covers. Even so, I continued to shiver. Throughout the early night I kept piling blankets on the bed until I had twelve piled up. (There was a reason there were so many blankets in the cabin!)

The covers seemed heavy enough, but they were not very warm. It was a little like piling boards on top of each other—heavy but not warm! Time and again I shivered myself to sleep that night. Finally, early in the morning when it was still dark, I decided to go outside to see if I could warm up by walking around. It actually felt warmer outside. Mark was up as well. We walked around listening to the birds waking up until it was time to go to the lodge to get our coffee and a breakfast snack.

The plan was to join a tour of four other people to see the elusive Resplendent Quetzal. At the crack of dawn we made our way into the forest where they had a nest. What a phenomenal time we had! We heard the bird but struggled to see it in the dense forest. Finally we saw a first-year male. By that time I was starting to warm up.

We watched the young male for some time while listening to the still-hidden mature male. Suddenly we saw the mature bird fly to a tree right beside us. It had an insect in its beak but seemed reluctant to go to its nest. Our guide explained that it was staying away from the nest until the young male leaves. We waited around for a while and then left. It was exhilarating to see it even though we did not see it feed its babies.

I have seen quetzals on three occasions now, but the excitement of seeing one has not lessened. Their great beauty and the fact that they are experts at staying hidden always makes it a challenge to see one. The best way to see them is to find their food source and then wait for them to arrive.

But you don't have to go outside the country to see birds. Go to your backyard and listen. If you cannot identify the bird songs, ask someone to help you. Every community has birdwatchers, or at least someone who knows one.

I used to be intimidated by "professional" birdwatchers, but I have learned that there is room for everyone. My way of birdwatching is merely different from theirs. My wife and I aren't into birdwatching to break records. We watch birds and photograph them for the pure pleasure of being outside and seeing birds.

We also enjoy scenery, plants, and wildlife. A few years ago we went on an extended western trip. We looked for birds, but it was not a priority. So do what you like and don't try to fit into someone else's agenda.

I suspect that many readers of this book are amateur photographers and birdwatchers like me. Being an amateur is not a bad thing. It can be a beginning to great things.

A Week to Remember

My wife Esther and I were at the Killbuck Marsh Wildlife Area in Ohio. As we walked down the wide path that used to be a road we heard a peculiar sound. It was very close and very loud. It sounded like an American Bittern that had gone to the Berkley School of Music but failed. It had the "oong" of the "oong'ka chunk" call of a bittern, but was louder.

We listened for a while but could not figure out what it was. It was in the marsh grass, so I assumed it was a rail. I decided to play a few rail songs from my birding app in hopes it would get curious and come into sight. First I played the Sora song without getting a rise from it. Next I played the Virginia Rail song. That brought the bird closer.

It kept coming closer and closer. We waited in silence for a while, then suddenly the bird stepped out of the grass beside the path. I quickly took a few pictures and tried to identify it. It was definitely not a Virginia Rail. But why had it responded? It looked more like the King Rail I had seen in Florida a few years earlier.

The next evening we were back at the marsh. As soon as we stepped out of the vehicle, we heard the rail again close to the bridge where we had seen it the evening before. A man stood there with a camera. When we got closer I asked the man if he had seen it yet, and he showed me a picture he had taken. At that moment the rail stepped out of the reeds and into the open. We both started taking pictures.

King Rail checking us out.

There was no doubt—it was a King Rail! What had thrown me off was that King Rails were not commonly seen in Ohio. I did find out later that almost every year one or more are sighted at the Killbuck Marsh.

When the man left, we watched the rail for a while, and then Esther went on down the path. After a few minutes I followed her. From then on things became a little unusual. I heard the rail down the path toward Esther, so I started walking a bit faster. When I saw movement in the grass, I quickly slowed to a stealthy walk. Suddenly the King Rail came out of the grass. It was following Esther!

It followed us the rest of the evening. Though it was interesting, it was also a bit unsettling. If you have never heard a King Rail, you cannot believe how loud it is at five feet. The whole time we were there, it didn't stop its "kek-brrr" call. It was a little like a beggar following us all evening begging for money.

On the bridge!

We went back to see the rail a number of times, and the same thing happened again. One particular evening we went back with our daughter Rachel. We stood around for a while but didn't hear anything. We missed it since it had become a friend by this time. I had said I would never play a King Rail song on my app again at that particular place. But Rachel wanted to see it. Should I? I did—once!

As soon as I played it, the rail responded right beside us as if to say, "I'm here. I'll be right out." And it was! Almost the whole time we were there it followed us in plain sight, only a few feet away. After I had crossed the bridge, I looked back to see Rachel on my side of the bridge and the rail close behind her on the bridge. We finally concluded that it was lonely, and for some reason it had decided we were the answer to its loneliness.

Esther and Rachel went ahead and out of sight. Since I had a sore leg I decided to stay where I was. The marsh was coming alive with night sounds, and I was enjoying every minute of it. A frog was sitting on a stump a little above the water. I watched it for a while. The daylilies were beautiful. Marsh Wrens were plentiful, and their raspy songs surrounded me.

Suddenly I saw something coming down the road. It was a raccoon and a deer. They were like two friends taking a stroll down the road. I kept watching as they slowly came my way. The deer stopped and ambled into the woods a short distance from me, but the raccoon kept coming.

Marsh Wren on a log.

Sometimes it disappeared behind the grass, sniffing at the water's edge but still coming my way. I stayed very quiet, sometimes looking away so as not to attract its attention.

Before long the raccoon was only twenty feet away and still coming toward me. It passed me about five feet away as I pretended not to be there. After it passed me, it suddenly looked back, wondering what I was. Clearly uneasy, it went into the tall grass and climbed up into the fork of a small tree about ten feet away.

By that time I saw the women coming back, so I called for them to hurry. The raccoon felt safe in the fork of the tree although it wasn't very high. After we took a few pictures we quietly left, bidding it a good night.

It had been an interesting evening.

The
Birds

King Rail

The King Rail is the largest North American rail. It is a beautiful bird about the size of a chicken. With its cinnamon breast, barred belly, and striped upperparts, it is designed to blend into the grasses. The King Rail is superb at hiding. But when disturbed, it can move quickly. Its compressed body, propelled by long stout legs, passes with great speed through the thickest growth of water plants. When forced to take wing, its flight is slow and clumsy.

It builds its nest among grasses or rushes, and the pile of dead cattails, marsh grass, or leaves that it gathers for this purpose is sometimes as much as twelve inches high. After nesting, the adults undergo a complete molt, losing all their flight feathers. For nearly a month they are unable to fly. During this time they stay well hidden. I would too!

Although the King Rail is not common in our area, we did have one last summer. Northern populations are migratory, while southern populations are generally year-round residents. I was surprised to learn that in some states these magnificent birds are still hunted. I would rather watch one with binoculars.

Being Useful

My first encounter with a King Rail was an experience I will not soon forget. It would come out of the tall grass for a little and then go back into cover again. I waited and watched. Finally it came out long enough for me to get a picture of it. After I took a picture, it bid me good day and went back home again, wherever that was. I never saw it again.

The King Rail isn't flashy like the colorful Purple Gallinule, but it serves a purpose just as much as the Purple Gallinule or any other bird or animal. All these creatures work together to keep nature balanced.

Did you ever think about that? Whatever your lot in life might be, believe that you are here for a purpose. Be cheerful and thank God for what He has done for you.

Be useful in your community and anywhere else you might be needed. Volunteer your time when a need arises. Being useful is a blessing to others as well as yourself.

Purple Gallinule

The Purple Gallinule is a shy bird that lives close to water, hiding in tall grasses. God has given this bird quite a talent. I have seen it swim like a duck but then walk like a chicken when it gets to floating plants. With its long toes, it can easily walk on the leaves and grass floating on the water.

Purple Gallinules often build their nests on rafts of floating vegetation. That way the nests can rise with the water level. Who do you suppose taught them to do that?

Purple Gallinules find shelter among tall grasses. These plants also provide much of their food. I have watched them climb up tall alligator flag plants to eat the seeds. As they get to the top of the plant, their weight makes the reeds bend over so they can go to the next reed and do it all over again.

These birds live primarily in the southern states but sometimes stray farther north during the summer. If you ever see one of these beautiful birds, take a moment to thank God. They are so pretty with their purple color. I looked for years before I saw one close enough to photograph.

Gentleness

The Purple Gallinule reminds me of people who are quiet and gentle. They go about their business without trying to be noticed and are a little reserved. Being quiet and a little shy fills a great need in a boisterous world.

Some people think they have to tell everyone they meet about everything they know. Others know a lot but say little. I have spoken to people who are not talkative, but when you take an interest in them you can be blessed by what you learn from them.

Be like the gallinule—go about your business in a pleasant and gentle way. Don't worry if you don't always know what to say when you are with other people. Most people who talk a lot don't learn as much as those who are quiet. Sometimes it is best to keep your ears open and your mouth closed. Walk quietly and you will be amply rewarded. You might even see a Purple Gallinule!

Limpkin

Limpkins are rarely seen in a flock but usually live a secluded life in pairs. They are known as the "crying bird" because of their peculiar wailing cries, both in the daytime and at night. Though they are fascinating birds, their constant wailing cry has a tendency to grind on a person after a while.

The Limpkin eats snails, especially the large, greenish apple snails. With its crooked bill it can reach into a snail shell and pull out the snail. It has a unique gap in its bill when it is closed, which helps to extract the snail from its shell. It is fascinating to watch them eat these snails.

It is difficult to make Limpkins fly. When they do take wing, they only go a short distance before dropping back into the shelter of the reeds. They have a peculiar limping gait, which is how they got their name.

It is a resident throughout Florida. The nest is a loosely constructed platform of sticks, leaves, grass, and moss, located a few feet from the ground in tangled underbrush or vines.

Understanding God's Plan

The Limpkin is quite plentiful in Florida, so it is easy to get tired of its peculiar, persistent cry. It also has a kind of tiresome twitching. It is not an easy bird for me to enjoy. Look at its drab color. It doesn't come close to the Painted Bunting or the Rose-breasted Grosbeak. But does color really matter? Does it matter if it has a peculiar twitch that makes it look like it is limping? Does it matter that it cannot sing like an oriole or a warbler?

What matters is that the Limpkin was designed by God. That makes it good. You too are God's creation. He has a plan for you. You might not know what that plan is right now, but don't wear yourself out worrying about it.

The best way to know and understand God's plan for your life is to commit yourself into His hands every day. Have a good attitude and be faithful in your home, in the church, and at work. As you yield to God, your relationship with Him will grow.

Sandhill Crane

Sandhill Cranes are widespread in the western two-thirds of North America. They grow up to four feet tall. Their wingspan is six to seven feet. They are quite the long-wings!

The red on their heads is actually a bald area. Many people think they have red feathers on their head, but they don't. They enjoy spending the night in wet areas, where they feel safe. During the day they go out to fields and eat grain, as well as small frogs, toads, grasshoppers, and other insects.

Sandhill Cranes are familiar birds in Florida and live there year round. They also spend summers in the north. More and more are coming to large freshwater marshes in Ohio. I greet them with a big howdy, and then I go my way and they go theirs. They are very friendly birds. By walking slowly and quietly, I have come within ten feet of them in the wild.

The male and female help each other build their nest. The nests are usually in marshes or bogs, though occasionally on dry land. Both parents help to incubate the two eggs. The chicks are able to leave the nest within a day after they hatch.

Being Polite

We should learn from the Sandhill Crane and respect others. When they fly in to join a flock on the ground, they approach quietly, but the ones on the ground call out a greeting to them. After they land, they talk bird talk to one another.

Don't be boisterous in your approach to others. Approach quietly and you will be appreciated for your quietness. Be friendly and you will gain friends. Take an interest in others; learn their likes and dislikes. Ask them about their family and where they live, where they go to school, or where they work. As you take an interest in their lives, they will take an interest in yours. Soon a friendship is established, often for life.

Being polite is godly. The Bible tells us to do to others as we would want them to do to us. I encourage you to adopt this motto and live by it. Never make fun of others or wish bad things for them. Treat them with great respect.

Black-necked Stilt

The Black-necked Stilt has extremely long, bright red legs. It wades through the water to catch food. Its large spearlike bill is specially designed to catch prey. Male Black-necked Stilts are a pretty black and white, as shown. The females and young are browner. Stilts are poor swimmers and generally feed in shallow water, searching out aquatic insects and their larvae. Strong and swift on the wing, they twist as they fly, alternately showing their black upper parts and white surfaces beneath.

Though they mostly live in the Gulf States and southern California, they are spreading north in the United States. They are rare on the Atlantic Coast. In winter, they go south as far as northern South America.

My wife Esther and I were walking along a swampy area when we came upon dozens of these birds in the company of egrets and herons. The stilts did not seem to mind our presence very much. We studied them for a time. They are active birds, walking a few steps, sticking their long beaks into the water, and then quickly moving forward to do it all over again.

Work and Rest

Just as the Black-necked Stilt wades into the water to find food, you must wade into life to find opportunity. The stilt doesn't waver, and you shouldn't either. Have a purpose and make sure you are serious about fulfilling that purpose. Be strong in God's will and overcome the world.

This bird is not fancy. It has only three colors: black and white with red legs. Isn't it surprising that black and white can be so beautiful? It is the way these two colors are arranged that makes it beautiful. The same goes for two of the stilt's attributes: work and rest. We need to work, but we must also not forget to rest.

Maybe you are discouraged and think you do not have the talents others do, and you have to work too hard. Learn to work diligently, but also learn to rest. Simply be a tool in the hands of God and make the best of what you have. Be busy, but be careful to not be consumed by your busyness.

American Woodcock

Walking quietly through a moist area overgrown with short saplings and brush, I was surprised to come upon this American Woodcock. I stopped and slowly brought up my camera. The bird gave me just enough time to photograph it before it flew away.

What an unusual bird! Look at its long bill. It is its boring tool to dig in soft mud for worms. The tip of the bill is flexible and can be opened while probing underground. This allows it to snatch any worms or larvae it finds.

These birds have a massive appetite, thanks to a super-fast digestive system. As a result, a woodcock can eat its weight in worms in one day. Wow, think how many hamburgers it would take if we did that!

During courtship, the males will climb in circles up to 300 feet, then drop to the ground in a zigzag dive. During the display, they make twittering sounds by air rushing through the wingtips. They generally do this right at dusk.

With its large eyes located near the top of the head it can watch for danger in the sky as it probes for food in the soil. God has given the American Woodcock exactly what it needs to survive.

Accepting Our Circumstances

Having what we need is not the same as having what we want. If we can learn to tell the difference, we will be happier throughout life.

Sometimes we might question why we are not like other people. Maybe others seem to have more physical abilities, be smarter, or be able to make more money. We have all been wonderfully created, but God has not made us all the same. Some things in life cannot be changed, such as how we look or what family we are born into. These are things we must accept.

We can choose to accept what we cannot change, or we can choose to be miserable and bitter. Life is much easier if we accept those things that we cannot change. We cannot constantly complain about how tough life is and still be happy. We must learn to accept what we have and who we are.

American Bittern

The American Bittern is a fascinating bird in the heron family, about 28 inches tall. Found in bogs and marshes, it is a master of camouflage. It is famous for its habit of "freezing." I watched one of these birds in tall grass with neck stretched out and head tilted back so that its beak was pointed straight up. It swayed slightly, mimicking the grass as it moved with the wind. I looked away for a moment, and when I looked back I had a problem finding it again. It blended in so perfectly with its surroundings.

The male makes a peculiar "oonk-a chunk, oonk-a-chunk" pumping call during the nesting season. When it does this, it bends its neck and then snaps it straight again! This unusual call has earned it the nickname "thunder-pumper."

Its nest consists of a grass-lined hollow in tufts of grass or turf in the middle of bogs or marshes, where it lays three or four plain brownish eggs. It nests in the northern parts of the United States and up into Canada. Its winters are spent in the southern United States and Central America.

Loving God's People

This American Bittern reminds me of people who blend in—some with the people of God and some with the worldly crowd. Some people like to blend in with the world while they profess to be Christians. Jesus said that if we are ashamed of Him, He will be ashamed of us. We cannot expect to be friends with the world and then have Jesus receive us into His kingdom.

We are called to love God and confess Christ as our Savior and Lord. Let's not put it off; life is short and eternity very long. Let's make the choice to blend in with the people of God. Let's be at peace with God and His people. That is the best kind of life.

Think about what Joshua shared with the people in Joshua 24:15: "As for me and my house, we will serve the LORD." Choose to blend in with God's people and you will be blessed.

Great Blue Heron

The Great Blue Heron has hidden beauty in its feathers. At first glance this bird may seem kind of drab, but it isn't. It even has a feather in its cap! These four-foot-tall birds are very handsome. The young birds are somewhat duller in color and take several years to attain their adult plumage. Great Blue Herons are quite common over most of North America.

In flight, herons carry their head drawn in against the shoulders, with the neck curved in an "S" shape. Great Blue Herons are shy birds and quickly fly off when approached. It is really difficult to sneak up on them. Their nests are a platform of sticks. They are placed in the tops of tall trees in rookeries of up to several hundred nests.

Great Blue Herons have special feathers on their chest that continually grow and fray into a powder. The herons collect this powder and use it like a washcloth to remove fish slime and other oils from their feathers as they preen. They like to eat small fish, shrimp, or aquatic insects. I have also watched them eat rather large fish. They just gulp them down, headfirst.

Community

Herons like to live together in one big community. In a community we learn how to listen, love, and live in harmony. We also learn patience, endurance, and how to work out issues.

The heron is always alert to danger. This is important when living in a community. But we should also encourage one another. The Bible tells us to "bear one another's burdens, and so fulfill the law of Christ."[1]

Living together in a community brings security. It is comforting. When someone has a need, the others jump in to help. We should try to live in peace with one another and not compete with one another about who is the greatest. Let's get along like the herons, not preferring certain people and disliking others.

As you live in your community, remember to focus on the good of everyone. Don't set your mind on high things that divide, but associate with the humble.

---

[1] Galatians 6:2

Great Egret

The Great Egret is often seen looking for something to eat as it wades through the marsh. It picks out a spider here and a bug there. It also eats minnows and even little frogs. It has beautiful plumes growing from the middle of its back.

In the late 1800s, these birds were killed in great numbers for those plumes, which were used to decorate ladies' hats. Thousands of egrets were slaughtered every summer. The poachers cut off their wings and left their bodies to rot among the nests in the rookeries. Agents hired men to do the dirty work and paid sky-high prices. By the year 1900 over five million birds of various species were being slaughtered annually. Thankfully, laws were eventually passed to protect them, and egrets are now quite plentiful through much of the warmer parts of the United States.

These shy, beautiful birds like to build their nest in colonies with other egrets and herons. A cluster of their nests is known as a rookery. At the Venice Rookery in Florida, Great Egrets, Snowy Egrets, Black-crowned Night Herons, and many other birds build their nests close together. There are perhaps fifty nests in a small area about half the size of our house.

Pride

God wants us to know that He loves each one of us, but He doesn't want us to think we are worth more than others. Do you look in the mirror and admire yourself? The egret is beautiful, but it doesn't show off.

The Bible tells us in Romans 12:3 to not think of ourselves more highly than we ought to think, but to think soberly. We should not praise ourselves. We are just normal people and have nothing to boast about. If others praise us, let's remain humble. Our calling in life is not to compete against others, but to work with others to glorify God.

Pride can blind you to who you really are and will affect your relationship with others. People who are humble are appreciated much more than those who are proud. Be humble and know that you are just like all the rest of us.

Snowy Egret

As you can see in the picture, the Snowy Egret is pure white. The long, flowing plumes on the back, head, and breast speak of great elegance. Egrets get their name from the French word *aigrette,* which means a spray of feathers.

How do you like its yellow booties? They're nice, aren't they? Another egret similar to this one is the Cattle Egret. The Cattle Egret, however, has a yellow bill and black feet.

I think the Snowy Egret is the most beautiful of all the egrets. It is especially beautiful during the nesting season. The male displays by pointing his bill straight up, raising his plumes, and pumping his head up and down while calling. It has an elegance of royalty about it.

Sometimes it can be seen walking through shallow water and stirring up the mud with its feet, hoping to flush out prey. It makes its nest in swamps, usually in company with other small herons.

Because of its beauty, it has suffered greatly from plume hunters. In 1886, the plumes from this bird were valued at $32 an ounce, twice the price of gold.

Greed

The Snowy Egret doesn't know how beautiful it is. It goes about its business of finding food and raising young without a thought of its beauty. It doesn't like when I get too close. I would never hurt it, but it doesn't know that. It has an inborn sense of survival and is suspicious of people like me. And rightly so! People like me hounded it almost to extinction in times past.

Although Snowy Egrets are now protected, that has not always been the case. Many years ago, some greedy men even murdered a game warden to acquire some rare egret plumes.

Greed makes people do wrong things. I know you wouldn't kill anyone, and I hope you wouldn't harm someone to get what you want. But what about cheating? Do you ever cheat to win a game? Do you lie in order to get away with things? What about stealing? These are all things people do because they are greedy.

Please treat everyone nicely. This Snowy Egret says, "Thank you for being nice!"

Little Blue Heron

The Little Blue Heron is most abundant in the Gulf States, only rarely straying as far north as New England. It is at home in impenetrable swamps where only birds or reptiles can tread with safety.

The head and neck of the Little Blue Heron is a nice rusty blue, with the rest of the plumage a dark slate-blue. During the summer, it has plumes on its head, breast, and back. Young birds are white for the first year, usually with only a tinge of blue on the forehead and the ends of the wings.

One day I noticed lots of herons and egrets flying in and out of some tall grasses in the middle of a swampy area. My curiosity was aroused, so I walked gingerly through the mostly dried up swamp. When I got to the tall reeds, I bent over and quietly made my way as close as I dared. Slowly I parted the grasses and almost gasped in awe. Little Blue Herons, Snowy Egrets, Great Egrets, and Roseate Spoonbills were at a tiny body of water. I had seldom seen Little Blue Herons before and was awed at how close I was to them. Eventually I backed away and left them to their secret hideaway.

Intense Living

See how alert this fellow is as he looks for breakfast. Sometimes you'll see a heron folding its wings over its eyes like you place your hand over your eyes to keep out the sun. That way it can see into the water better. They look intently into the water so they don't miss an opportunity.

Be like the Little Blue Heron and be intense. When something needs to be done, do not look around to see if someone else will do it. Just jump in and do it. Do not be distracted by unprofitable things. Be intense and intentional.

Multitasking is doing several things at the same time. This has not been proven to be very productive. It is better to do the one thing at hand and do it well. Do it heartily as unto the Lord. Do not let an opportunity pass you by. Remember, an opportunity missed is often gone forever.

Reddish Egret

The Reddish Egret is a medium-sized heron. The head and neck, including the pinions on its neck and breast, are reddish-brown. The rest of the plumage is mostly gray. There is also a white morph of this bird.

Their food consists of small fish, frogs, lizards, insects, and mice. They will stand motionless in shallow water for a long time waiting for their prey. Woe to the creature that comes within striking distance of their spear-like bill!

I watched a Reddish Egret fishing in a saltwater pool. It stirred the ground with its feet and raised its wings up and apart so it could see better into the water. It has the same effect as when we place our hand above our eyes to block out the sun.

Their flight is strong and graceful as they make their way from where they raise their young to their feeding grounds on the mudflats left bare by the receding tide. They mainly nest in the Gulf Coast States, as far north as South Carolina.

Being Focused

The Reddish Egret is a joy to see. I have only ever seen two. One was with a large group of shorebirds, while the other was in a saltwater pool off the shore. Both stood apart from the other herons in both their mannerisms and their beauty.

Do you stand out because you are a person who is focused on doing the right thing? This bird did not ask to be an attraction. Indeed, it didn't know that it was. Can you do the same? Just go about your business and don't think about being an attraction.

People often beg for attention. They want to do things bigger, better, and sometimes more weird than others. It is a special delight to see a young man or woman serve the Lord with earnestness, not minding the things of the world. Be that kind of person. Focus on what you can do for Christ. Read your Bible to learn how you can serve God better. Paul wrote that we are to "press toward the mark for the prize of the high calling of God in Christ Jesus."[1] This speaks about being focused, so stay focused on Christ.

---

[1] Philippians 3:14

Green Heron

The Green Heron, at only seventeen inches, is our smallest heron. In its spring plumage, it is a beautiful bird. It is found in marshes, along creeks, or about the edges of shallow ponds or lakes.

Green Herons are often seen sitting on a partly submerged log sunning themselves or waiting for a tempting frog or fish to pass by. They sometimes place small twigs or insects in the water as bait to attract fish. They wait silently, not moving an inch, staring intently into the water. When a little fish comes by, the heron snatches it with lightning speed.

When Green Herons are among rushes, they attempt to escape observation by mimicking their surroundings, and they do so very successfully. When they are alarmed, their dark cap is raised into a short crest. As they take flight, they often utter a single sharp shriek.

This bird builds a stick nest in a tree, where it lays its two to six pale bluish-green eggs. Unlike most herons and egrets, it likes to be alone—just mother and father tending to the family. It nests in the eastern half of the United States. Not all Green Herons migrate; some are year-round residents in the southern states.

Patience

I like the colors on the Green Heron. When the sun hits it just right, the colors come out in all their brilliancy.

This little heron often sits quietly on a limb just above the surface of the water as it waits patiently for its supper. When it sees a little fish or frog, it lowers its head and then quietly sticks out its neck until it is within striking distance. Then, like a bolt of lightning, it strikes. As soon as it has eaten its food, it settles back again and waits for the next meal. It does this many times a day. It never seems in a hurry. It has an inborn sense of patience.

Unfortunately, most of us don't have an inborn sense of patience. It is something we need to learn. Sometimes it takes years to learn that patience is a valuable virtue. If we can learn patience and wisdom, we have learned something that many people never learn.

White Ibis

It looks like these White Ibises have something on their mind. I believe it is food. Look at their long, sharp bills. As they wade in the water, they sweep their bills back and forth in search of prey. They like to pick up crabs, crayfish, little frogs, small fish, or other tiny marine creatures.

White Ibises are about two feet tall, with a wingspan of about three feet. They have a loud, harsh croak. When the babies are hatched, their beaks are straight, but after about two weeks their bills start curving downward. The young birds have brownish-gray feathers. As they reach adulthood, their feathers slowly turn white except for some black on the bottom of their wings. When they fly you can see their black wingtips, making them very beautiful in flight.

The White Ibis is abundant in the southern states, where it makes its poorly made nest of twigs or rushes in immense rookeries in remote swamps. Male White Ibises are extremely protective of their nest and jealously guard the female.

Relationships

I never saw a White Ibis until I got to Florida. I thought they looked really strange with their red bills and red legs. But I no longer think of them as strange. I have seen them often and gotten to know them. That's the key in relationships. Once we really get to know people, we look at them differently.

There's an old Indian saying: "Do not judge your brother until you have walked a mile in his moccasins." That's good advice. Withhold judgment until you get to know people. It is so easy to misjudge a person's motives.

Years ago there was a man who was known to be quite poor. Rumor was that he was misusing his money. After he died, it was discovered that he had been giving money to needy widows every month. Let's think twice before we gossip about people or slander them. They might be doing better things than we are.

The next time you see someone who seems a little strange, don't be too quick to pass judgment. Instead, learn to know the person. Things may not be as they appear.

Roseate Spoonbill

The Roseate Spoonbill is named for its unusual spoon-shaped bill, which it uses to scoop up all kinds of goodies out of the water. The spoonbill stands about thirty inches tall.

Take a look at its pretty colors. I see a tinge of yellow, maybe a little green, some orange, and lots of pink. And the legs are red. The head of the adult is entirely bald. The Roseate Spoonbill eats crustaceans and other aquatic creatures that contain pigments called carotenoids. These pigments give them their pink color. The same goes for the flamingo.

Spoonbills nest in the Gulf States, particularly Florida and southern Texas. They travel and nest in groups. When they fly, their flight is strong and their neck is fully extended. They slowly beat the air with their large wings. This is one bird I have never heard make a sound.

We were driving down a road in Florida when we saw a large flock of these birds on a riverbank. We found a place to park our vehicle, then walked back to where we had seen the birds. When we got through the woods to the riverbank we were amazed. Over one hundred Roseate Spoonbills were on the other side of the river preening themselves. It was a sight to behold.

God's Design

The first time I saw a Roseate Spoonbill, I thought it looked awkward with its strange bill. But I soon saw that God did not make a mistake—the bill is exactly the tool the spoonbill needs. When a spoonbill walks through the water, it sweeps its partly opened bill back and forth to search for food. When it finds something, it quickly scoops it up.

God also did not make a mistake when he made you. It doesn't matter where you were born or how you look, God has a purpose for you. Do not ask God why He made you the way He did, but be available for His service.

Do not try to compete with others, but work with them. Forget about your inabilities and make yourself available to others. God has a purpose for you. Let Him work out the details.

Osprey

The Osprey loves to fish. It has fish for breakfast, fish for lunch, and fish for dinner—every day. Its flight is graceful and sweeping. It circles above the water until it sees a fish, then it descends with great speed into the water. It often disappears for a few seconds but soon emerges with its struggling victim grasped in its powerful talons. It does this again and again, especially when it has hungry young ones to tend. Ospreys are the only raptors that dive into water.

The Osprey's feet have barbed pads to help it keep a firm grip on a fish. When it catches a fish, it rotates it in mid-air to carry it headfirst. Apparently it knows something about aerodynamics!

An Osprey's nest is generally quite large. It is made of sticks of various sizes, with grasses spun throughout. Other smaller birds have been known to build their nests around the edges of their nests! Surprisingly, they all live together in harmony.

It is interesting to listen to Ospreys "talk" to one another. They make chirping sounds. If you listen closely, you can hear variations in their chirps. I wonder at times what they talk about.

Humility

The Osprey is a bird I enjoy watching. It is exciting to watch one dive into the water to catch a fish. An Osprey flew over me recently with a good-sized fish. It didn't fly over me so I could marvel at its catch. It does not fish so it has something to brag about, but so it has something to eat.

You might be successful in what you do, but do not try to attract attention. The Osprey doesn't. Go about your life with great expectations in a humble way. God might have great things for you to do, or it might be something small and insignificant. It really does not matter, as long as you do it to the glory of God.

Look for opportunities to serve people and God. When you see an opportunity, think about the Osprey, and do not hesitate. Dive into the work. Catch the biggest fish, or do the best work you can, then give God the glory.

Bald Eagle

The Bald Eagle is a handsome bird of prey and can be seen all across the United States and Canada. The eagle is the national symbol of the United States. Benjamin Franklin argued against the choice of the Bald Eagle as the national emblem. He considered it a bird of bad moral character because it sometimes steals prey from other birds.

The Bald Eagle is one of the largest birds in North America and has a wingspan of up to six feet. To see one is something to talk about. It likes to be near streams or lakes, where it eats fish, ducks, and small mammals.

Not far from our house are two eagle nests that we enjoy looking at through our spotting scope. One of the nests is in a heron rookery with fifty to sixty heron nests. The eagles and herons seem to get along well. The huge eagle nest sets it apart from the much smaller heron nests.

At one time Bald Eagles were becoming very scarce. This was due to chemicals that farmers put on their fields. It made the eagle's eggs thin-shelled, so they often broke during incubation. When the chemicals were banned, the eggshell became stronger and didn't break. I hope we learned a lesson from that.

Purpose

Daniel purposed in his heart that he would not defile himself. When temptations came, he would not yield. He stood firm, but he paid a price to do so. The world needs to see young people who are strong in heart and in purpose.

The Bald Eagle is big, powerful, and beautiful. To see this big bird with its white head and tail glide through the air is truly breathtaking. Seeing godly young men and women who claim high morals in the midst of an immoral society is also breathtaking. To see them study hard in school and obey their parents is admirable and breathtaking. Seeing young men and women who are powerful in their character is like seeing an eagle!

Be strong and of good courage. When you are strong in integrity the world will notice. Stand straight and do not waver. Soar through life like the eagle, with majesty and purpose, high above the world.

Red-shouldered Hawk

The Red-shouldered Hawk is an attractive, medium-sized hawk. It has rich, reddish-brown shoulders and underparts. Young birds are duller, with streaked whitish underparts. It is very vocal, and can be heard screeching "kee-ah, kee-ah, kee-ah" as it flies overhead. It is a call that is easily recognizable.

Red-shouldered Hawks live throughout most of the eastern United States, mainly in heavily forested areas. In recent years they have become more common and can sometimes be found in suburban areas.

In courtship, the male Red-shouldered Hawk displays by flying upward, calling, and then diving steeply. Pairs may soar together in circles, calling—even flying upside down for short distances!

Red-shouldered Hawks feast on moles and field mice, as well as grasshoppers and an occasional rabbit and squirrel. I have seen them flying to the grass to pick up large grubs. Their nest, made of sticks, is used over and over. Crows are the most common threat to their eggs.

The Red-shouldered Hawk and the American Crow have a love-hate relationship. They sometimes chase each other and steal food from one another. At other times, however, they join forces to chase off owls.

Blessing Your Community

Many people look at hawks as a nuisance bird that preys on chickens and birds. They do that occasionally, but it is usually not a major part of their diet. Hawks do much good by controlling the vermin that can carry diseases. They also eat snakes that many people do not like. You could say they are community workers.

We also need to be known as people who work for the community. We are not to be selfish. We have been called to help each other. Just like the hawks, we help keep the community clean. Let's strive to be honest and upright—to do a day's work at fair wages and charge fair prices for whatever we sell. Being productive citizens is one way to help the community.

Every community has a great need for people who are unselfish—people who share the love of God by loving other people. Be a blessing in your community by spreading God's love.

Swainson's Hawk

The Swainson's Hawk is primarily a bird of the western United States and Canada. In the fall it migrates south to spend the winter in South America. It likes open grasslands and desertlike habitats. It is common to see it sitting on electric poles or fence posts. It can sometimes be seen on large hay bales watching for something to eat.

Swainson's Hawks have a variety of plumages. The bird in the picture is a light-morph bird, which is by far the most common. It has a band of rich chestnut across the breast, giving it a hooded look.

These hawks have one of the longest migrations of any North American raptor, sometimes flying all the way to Argentina. Their flight from the nesting ground to the South American pampas in southern Brazil or Argentina can be as long as 7,100 miles. They migrate in "kettles"[1] of hundreds or thousands. I once saw kettle after kettle migrating in Central America. There must have been a thousand birds total. It was a sight I will never forget.

Being Alert

This Swainson's Hawk is looking for a meal. It likes mice, rabbits, and even snakes. It has eyes that can see better than we can and sharp claws to snatch food. This hawk is watching for an opportunity to snatch breakfast. Its eyes are open. It is alert. It is intent.

The Bible tells us to "continue in prayer, and watch in the same with thanksgiving."[2] We are also told to watch, for we do not know what hour the Lord comes. We must not get caught up with the trivial things of this world, but watch faithfully for Christ's return. Be a serious young person who knows that the serious things of life reap more benefits than the foolishness of the world.

Be alert when you work so you don't get hurt. Be alert when you drive down the road. Be alert to danger of any kind, but be especially alert to recognize dangers that could lead you astray spiritually. Also be alert to opportunity—a chance to help someone, to speak a kind word of encouragement, or just to be a good example.

---

[1] A kettle is a group of birds circling together in a warm air thermal, usually during migration.
[2] Colossians 4:2

Crested Caracara

The Crested Caracara is a peculiar bird. The name *caracara* comes from the bird's call, but most of the time it is silent. Is the caracara a vulture or a hawk? It has habits that resemble both, and in South America it is sometimes called the Mexican Eagle. Although the food of this bird is largely carrion, it will catch and eat small mammals, fish, worms, and insects. Caracaras are more quarrelsome than vultures and frequently fight over their prey.

The first time I saw this bird was in Texas. I didn't know what it was until later when I looked it up in a bird guide. A few years later I heard that caracaras were also present in Florida. We spent hours in central Florida until we eventually saw one. They now seem more plentiful. They can often be seen in an open field walking about searching for food or standing erect on branches or fence posts.

The caracara's range is primarily in Central and South America, reaching only as far north as the southernmost states in the United States.

A Willing Worker

Crested Caracaras are like vultures in that they are part of God's cleanup crew. They clean up all the dead animals. Recently I told a man who drives a garbage truck that he has a very important job. Cleaning up is important, as a dirty environment can lead to diseases. You might not be involved with cleaning up, but you might have a job that you consider unimportant.

Maybe you think your job is not as important as some, but usually a task is as important as we consider it to be. Do every job with your whole heart. Don't wait on great things to come your way. Do the small things first in order to get to the more important ones. Any job is worth doing well.

You should consider it a privilege to do well what you are called to do. Give attention to detail, and it will be a testimony to others. Grumbling and complaining makes everything seem harder, while smiling and being thankful makes it easier.

Greater Roadrunner

The Greater Roadrunner lives in the southwestern United States. It likes the desert where it can easily find lizards and other creepy, crawly things to eat. Though it can fly, it prefers running. If you ever see a bird running down the road at twenty miles per hour trying to catch a lizard, you can safely assume it's a roadrunner! They are fun to watch. These skinny, long-tailed birds are fairly large and can measure up to 24 inches.

One thing I like about roadrunners is that they mate for life. Usually they nest only in the spring, but sometimes there is a second nesting in August and September. They eat grasshoppers, mice, lizards, and even snakes.

Obviously, the people of New Mexico like this bird since it is their state bird! Maybe one reason they like it is because it eats poisonous rattlesnakes. The bird darts in and out as it pecks at the rattlesnake. Eventually the snake tires and the roadrunner jumps on the snake's head and holds it down as it pecks away. Sometimes it bashes the snake's head against a rock to kill it.

Sometimes it leaps straight up from the ground to snatch flying prey. They have been seen catching hummingbirds this way.

Taking the Initiative

Would you like living in the desert where the temperature can rise to 120°F? The roadrunner doesn't mind. It doesn't sit around worrying about the heat.

Be like the roadrunner and be a hustler. Though the roadrunner is a fast runner, it doesn't run all the time. It is also observant, looking for prey. Learn from this bird that it really is the early bird that gets the worm! Don't lag behind. Take the initiative and do quickly what needs to be done without being told. The world needs to see young people who take responsibility.

Taking the initiative means you are able to assess something and act upon it. As you go through life you will sometimes have to make crucial decisions. The best way to make these decisions is to pray and learn from those who have experience. Discuss issues with your parents and other Christian brothers and sisters. Take the initiative, but also learn to observe before you run!

Yellow-billed Cuckoo

The Yellow-billed Cuckoo is one of my favorite birds. I tracked down this bird in Texas in a wooded area in the middle of an open field. I had never been this close to a cuckoo before. It was a great joy to be able to see it at close range. I hear this bird more often than I see it since it likes to sit high in a tree and remain hidden by leaves.

Curiously enough, while the main food of the cuckoo is insects, it also eats tree frogs. And it is one of the few birds that actually enjoys eating those nasty tent caterpillars. It can eat up to a hundred at one sitting!

The Yellow-billed Cuckoo spends the summer in the eastern United States and migrates to South America for the winter. The male helps incubate the eggs. He is generous to his mate and takes the night shift. It is common to find little ones of several sizes in the same nest. There may be one nearly grown, another just beginning to get feathers, and a third not yet out of the egg.

According to folklore, when the cuckoo sings rain is not far behind. I debunk that as superstition since I often hear the cuckoo, and it has nothing to do with rain.

Focusing on Others

If you listen carefully, you can hear the Yellow-billed Cuckoo's soft cluck in the morning as it talks to other cuckoos. They like to talk to each other just like we do. They establish relationships when they communicate. That's also how we make friends, isn't it?

When you feel like you need attention, remember the Yellow-billed Cuckoo hidden among the leaves eating tiny caterpillars. It is happy as it clucks to others.

We are better off if we are not the center of attention. Instead, let's put our focus on others, looking for opportunities to brighten their days.

The Bible says we are to draw close to God and He will draw close to us. That's fellowship with Him. When that happens, God will give us a "soft cluck" to minister to others. Isn't that a wonderful thought? See what you can do for others.

Burrowing Owl

The Burrowing Owl has long legs, a short tail, and no ear tufts. Standing only about ten inches tall, this owl lives in Florida and in the prairie regions west of the Mississippi.

In the prairies, Burrowing Owls live in the same habitat as prairie dogs and use their deserted burrows as nests. However, the owls do not live peaceably in the same burrows with the prairie dogs. In fact, the owls sometimes feed on young prairie dogs. They also eat rodents, small snakes, and birds.

Besides prairie dog tunnels, Burrowing Owls also use the burrows of woodchucks, foxes, and tortoises. The burrows are up to ten feet long, with a nesting chamber at the end. Sometimes, especially in Florida where there are no prairie dogs, they build their own burrows.

Burrowing Owls are both diurnal and nocturnal, doing most of their hunting after dusk but often sitting at the mouth of the burrow during the daytime. They have a wide range of calls. When threatened by predators, they go into their burrows and scare off their enemies by mimicking the sound of a rattlesnake.

A Cheerful Attitude

I have wondered why these owls choose to live in a hole like a prairie dog or a groundhog. The only thing I can think of is that the Creator made them that way.

Maybe you feel a little different than others. Maybe you have some disability and can't do what others can. Many years ago I visited a man who had been in an accident. As a result, he could move only his head. There he lay day after day while his family took care of him. I was impressed by how cheerful the whole family was. Even the paralyzed young man was cheerful. He laughed and told stories. He set the tone for a joyful evening. Their secret was that they had accepted what had happened.

You see, even though the Burrowing Owl has its nest in a hole, it is still an owl. It cheerfully lives the way God created it. Even if you can't do what others can, you can focus on your abilities and how you can do them well. Go for it.

Red-headed Woodpecker

The Red-headed Woodpecker wears a red cap, a white shirt, and a black coat. It looks quite professional! It lives east of the Rocky Mountains. A couple years ago I thought Red-headed Woodpeckers were dying out since I rarely saw one. Now I see them often. They enjoy peanuts and bring their young to our homemade peanut feeder.

We watched as one of these woodpeckers hammered out a hole near the top of our peanut feeder. It was humorous to see it pick a peanut out of the feeder, then go to the top and drop it into the hole it had made. I guess that's one way of recycling!

One day I heard it pecking quite feverishly on the house. My wife said maybe it was telling me the peanuts were all gone. I checked the feeder and, sure enough, it was empty. A few days later I was sitting inside the window when the woodpecker starting drumming just outside at the edge of the roof. I looked up and saw it hanging upside down looking at me. I filled the feeder and all was well again!

Have you ever wondered why a woodpecker doesn't get a headache from all its pounding? There's a reason! God has designed the woodpecker's long tongue to fit inside a special cavity around the brain, cushioning it.

Being Authentic

Being ourselves is called being authentic. Don't try to be a copycat. Don't hang upside down like the woodpecker or do other silly acts for attention. Trying to be like someone else serves no good purpose.

Instead of wishing you were someone else, be yourself and focus on what you *can* do. Once you know what you can do, exercise that talent until you become good at it. But always stay humble. This way people will not only like what you do but who you are.

God wants you to use your talents to serve Him and the people around you. Be confident and bold, but not excessively so. Too much boldness can be devastating, and too little can stall you. Ask God and other people for direction, and you will know what is needed.

Red-bellied Woodpecker

The Red-bellied Woodpecker is about the size of the Red-headed Woodpecker. It lives east of the Rocky Mountains in woodlands. The red belly of this attractive bird is easy to miss, and many people never notice it. It has black-and-white stripes on its back, a little like a zebra.

Woodpeckers have rounded tails, which they use as braces. With its short legs and tail it braces itself as it pounds the tree for food. It is a little like a man who braces himself as he handles a jackhammer.

You will often see these birds going up and down the trunk of dead trees in search of worms and insects. For a Red-bellied Woodpecker, worms and insects are like ice-cream and chocolate cake on your plate. It also likes peanuts. We have a clear feeder attached to our dining room window where we place mixed feed that includes peanuts. We enjoy how they swoop in and land on the feeder as if they owned it.

They build their nests in cavities in dead trees. Some people think dead trees are eyesores and dangerous. The woodpeckers don't think so. Leave some standing for them! Chickadees, nuthatches, and bluebirds also use them for nests. So think about the birds, and dead trees will start looking nice.

Being a Testimony

The Red-bellied Woodpecker feeds freely on small acorns. It also likes peanuts. It can hang upside down without much effort. Have you ever tried that? If you do, please don't try to eat peanuts at the same time! The woodpecker here is getting a peanut out of a peanut feeder I made.

The Red-bellied Woodpecker is predictable. It has a peculiar call that immediately identifies it. The next time you are in the woods, listen for a bird calling "cha, cha, cha," and you will likely see this bird.

You should also live a life that immediately identifies you. Be the same person regardless where you are. Don't be cheerful when away from home and grouchy at home. Always be the same, and people will appreciate your sameness. Be a pleasant person who enjoys people.

Pileated Woodpecker

The crow-sized Pileated Woodpecker can be seen in heavily wooded areas across the eastern United States. I have also seen them in smaller tracts of woods. We even enjoy them at our feeders, though it is a rather wild and shy bird.

Pileated Woodpeckers nest primarily in dead trees, excavating a hole from 10-24 inches deep. These large cavities will sometimes be used by Wood Ducks in future seasons.

The male and female stay together on their territory all year round. A few years ago I found a nest and spent hours watching the adults feed their young. They did not seem to mind that I was only about thirty feet away. It was one of those rare moments with the birds.

The food of this bird consists of insects and various berries. They also love peanut butter suet. To prepare this, melt peanut butter with lard, then stir in some oatmeal, cornmeal, whole wheat flour, and a little sugar. The Pileated Woodpecker in this photograph seems to be telling me in no uncertain terms that it's time to get the feeder restocked.

Quiet Time

You usually know when you meet something unusual—like the Pileated Woodpecker. Seeing it up close is to see the beauty of God's creation.

The Pileated Woodpecker is shy but not soon spooked. One day I came upon one on a fallen tree. His attitude told me he was hungry, and if I didn't do anything rash he wouldn't either. He soon got busy hammering out worms, and I got busy watching. It was an incredible experience. The blows he struck to the wood were terrific. The noise of one at work can often be heard a quarter of a mile away or more.

You might not see this woodpecker up close, but I'm sure you've also had defining moments in nature that you won't soon forget. Be active and curious. Take time to ponder the usual as well as the unusual. See things that others miss. Most defining moments of life are made in times of quietness, so slow down and make some quiet moments for yourself. Doing so will prepare your heart to worship the One who made it all.

Scissor-tailed Flycatcher

The Scissor-tailed Flycatcher is a beautiful bird with its pale gray head, salmon-pink flanks, and dark gray wings. But what really sets it apart is its beautiful nine-inch-long, black and white forked tail. This flowing tail is the most conspicuous part of the bird when it flies, reminding one of a kite soaring gracefully in the March wind.

The Scissor-tailed Flycatcher is common in the Southern Great Plains and Texas. You rarely see only one since it likes the company of others of its kind. They often form large pre-migratory roosts in late summer, with up to a thousand birds in one flock.

I had a grand time on a narrow country road in eastern Texas. Scissor-tailed Flycatchers seemed to be everywhere. It was a lot of fun watching them catch insects. As soon as one caught something, it would fly to a fence and eat it. After it had eaten, it would sit for only a short time before it swooped through the air again. It reminded me of a person who hustles at his job.

The Scissor-tailed Flycatcher uses many human products in its nest, such as string, cloth, paper, carpet fuzz, and cigarette filters. The female hatches the eggs alone, while the male keeps watch nearby, sometimes bringing food to the female.

Compassion

When the female Scissor-tailed Flycatcher sits on the nest to incubate her eggs, the male does not just forget about her. Instead, he thinks about her needs. Not only is he busy chasing off potential enemies, but he remembers that she might be hungry and brings her food. That is compassion—thinking of others.

We too need compassion for others. We should be nice to everyone, but especially so to those who are suffering or are handicapped in some way.

We often take too much for granted. We should praise God when we are healthy. One way we can show God how thankful we are is to be compassionate toward people who are sick or handicapped. We can do that by visiting them or doing something for them. Remember that being compassionate is a testimony of your Christian faith.

Blue Jay

The Blue Jay is a rowdy fellow. He is the guardian of the forest. His loud call informs all the other birds that something is in the air—or on the ground! When he flies to the bird feeder, other birds scatter.

Blue Jays are known for their intelligence and complex social systems. I have often seen these birds gang up on a crow, or even a hawk, and chase it away.

In a process known as "anting," Blue Jays will rub an ant through their feathers before gobbling it down. It is uncertain why they do this, but two theories have been proposed. The first is that the formic acid the ant releases might be beneficial in controlling lice and other parasites on the Blue Jay's feathers. The second is that the ant simply tastes better without the acid!

Blue Jays sometimes pluck corn from the ear in rapid succession, storing the kernels in their mouth. They then fly off to store them in some secret place. They have tight family bonds, and when they feed among family members they lower their crests and feed peacefully.

Bullying

The Blue Jay comes boldly to the feeders because it is his nature to do so. He doesn't care if he interferes with others. He doesn't know anything about waiting for his turn. He is a bully. Do you identify with him? Are you rude? A bully? I hope not.

Do you ever make fun of others, laughing at their clothes or character traits that are different from yours? Please don't. God has made us in different ways. We need variety. Some people are weak in one area of life but strong in other ways.

Follow the Golden Rule and treat others as you would have them treat you. People who are picked on may not show their true feelings, but it does hurt them. So instead of picking on people, make them your friends. When you make friends, it makes you feel much better than if you mock them or bully them. Try it. Learn a good lesson and lower your crest!

Florida Scrub-Jay

The Florida Scrub-Jay lives only in Florida. As the name implies, it likes to live in areas with lots of shrubs. These offer protection from enemies and provide a place to build its nest.

The Florida Scrub-Jay is a friendly fellow and loves to be around his friends. Young birds often stay with the family group and help their parents raise the next year's brood. Studies show that parents with "helpers" successfully raise more young than others.

At one time these birds were quite numerous, but as more of its habitat was bulldozed for housing they diminished in numbers. Now the Florida Scrub-Jay is found in only a few places. Estimates are that only about 4,000 are left.

We were walking along a path in a state park in Florida when we saw this curious fellow. He came very close and watched us. It seemed he was trying to figure out if we were friend or foe. After a while some more came to check us out. We got a good look at them since they were only a few feet from us. Later my brother was along and one flew in and sat on his head!

Loving Your Enemies

You can look just as neat and confident as this jay, and I hope you do. But are you still miserable inside? Some young people think everyone is against them: their brothers and sisters, the pastor, and even their parents. This is usually not true, but sometimes bad things do happen to good people. I am sorry if you have been bullied, or other bad things have happened to you. It is not a good feeling.

As a young person I was bullied, but I learned a little secret: Smile at those who make your life miserable. It is no fun mocking those who smile. If you continue to be bullied or abused, tell someone. Please.

And don't forget what Jesus said about doing good to those who mistreat us. That's good advice. Maybe if someone takes something from you or is mean to you, you can do something nice in return. Take a lesson from the Florida Scrub-Jay. We can accomplish more if we are friendly and help each other.

Horned Lark

The Horned Lark can often be found year round on open ground or last year's cornfields, foraging for weed or grass seeds. This bird so perfectly blends into its surroundings that it is difficult to see when it is not moving. I have discovered that scanning an area with binoculars is the best way to find them. The "horns" on each side of its head are not really horns but tufts of feathers.

Though the Horned Lark's song is pretty, it is weak and can't be heard very far away. Horned Larks are most evident during the courtship period preceding nesting. The male flies up from the ground at a steep angle up to 800 feet high. After hovering or circling for a few minutes while uttering his distinctive, tinkling song, he pulls in his wings and plummets toward the earth, opening his wings just before landing.

The female builds her nest without any help from the male. It is quite an elaborate affair. First she digs a little cavity in the ground, then weaves a basket with grass. After lining it with fur or feathers, she often places a "doorstep" of pebbles beside it!

Unity and Humility

See how this Horned Lark blends into its surroundings? If you want to see it, go out into a plowed field in the springtime and watch for it. I have also seen it on cornstalks sticking out of the snow.

Sometimes we need to stand out from the crowd, but at other times we need to blend in. When the crowd is working toward some good thing, blend in. I like to think that being part of a fellowship is humility. Humility is a desire to blend in and not be noticed.

The Horned Lark finds its food in a plowed or bare field. A plowed field is not a beautiful or productive place, but this is where it was designed to live. I'm sure the Horned Lark has no complaints about this. I encourage you to enjoy your own plowed field, and then humbly submit to God.

Tufted Titmouse

The Tufted Titmouse is a common gray bird that inhabits all of the eastern United States. It likes to visit bird feeders in the winter to feast on sunflower seeds. It likes to carry the seeds away and store them for later use. Researchers studying chickadees, a close relative of titmice, have found that they can remember the hiding spot of thousands of seeds they have tucked away.

Titmice build their nests in old woodpecker cavities. They line their nest with soft grass, moss, and animal fur if they can find it. They have been seen plucking hairs from sleeping dogs and other animals—and even humans. The following was in a 1924 issue of *Bird-Lore:* "I was seated on a stump at the edge of the woods when a titmouse lit on my head, and began to pluck the hairs. The pricking of its sharp little toes on my scalp and the vigor of the hair-pulling was too much for my self-control, and I instinctively moved my head. Away it flew, but only for a moment, and then it was back at work, harder than before."

After the nesting season, titmice tend to stay close together as family units. They often associate in loose groups with other birds such as chickadees, sparrows, and cardinals. Occasionally a young titmouse helps care for the nestlings of the next year's brood.

Confidence

Titmice are happy and confident little things. They can fly from one tree to another as easily as we can walk on the ground.

To have confidence means you are certain of something. And because you are sure of it, that assurance becomes a powerful force in your life and you can do things. It enables you build the finest piece of furniture and gives meaning to the deepest thoughts and ideas of your heart.

Do you have confidence in yourself? Though a person can be overly confident, I'd like to encourage you to have confidence to accomplish your vision. For a Christian, confidence means you have an assurance that you can do the right thing. When you have that confidence, and you desire to please God, then do it.

Cactus Wren

The dry southwestern part of our country, from the lower Rio Grande Valley to the Pacific, is known as the cactus region. It is very arid and desolate. Sometimes it does not rain for many months. This is where the Cactus Wren lives.

The first time I saw Cactus Wrens was in southern Arizona. We watched them for quite some time as they flitted from plant to plant. They did not seem to mind our presence as I took multiple photos.

Cactus Wrens don't mind sitting on a sharp cactus. They seem as comfortable there as I am sitting in my chair! They even build their nests in these cactus plants. Maybe the sharp spines help protect the nest from predators that would harm the eggs. The nest is large and bulky, shaped a little like a football.

The Cactus Wren is large for a wren, measuring a little over eight inches. Cactus Wrens like to take a dust bath before they go to their nests. This helps reduce feather parasites and keeps their feathers looking good. They do not have to drink water to survive, getting all their liquid from juicy insects and fruit.

Being a Servant

Like the Cactus Wren, it is good for us to be content. When you feel like complaining about the "cactus needles" in your life, think about the wren sitting happily on the cactus.

You might think you do not have much opportunity, but if you look around you will see many opportunities to serve. When you are given work to do, do not look at how hard it is, but how you can do it best. Think about how you can use the abilities you have to be a faithful servant. Samson used the jawbone of a donkey to do what needed to be done. Aaron had a rod, and David had a staff. Use what you have and do it without complaining.

Tasks are easier when we have a good attitude. Be cheerful and the thorns of labor will become softer. Remember, "Whatsoever ye do, do it heartily, as to the Lord, and not unto men" (Colossians 3:23).

Veery

The Veery is a thrush found in the eastern United States and Canada. It can be found deep in the woods, often close to running water. It is a quiet and somewhat elusive bird.

A feeding Veery makes long jumps, flipping over leaves to find ants, bugs, beetles, or earthworms. Sometimes it quivers its foot on the ground. The vibrations of this unusual habit are thought to stir up insects for the bird to eat.

Veerys have been observed flying over a mile high during migration. They migrate at night, usually in small groups. They keep together in the dark by calling to each other as they fly. A Veery can travel up to 160 miles in one night! Studies reveal that unlike many birds that alternate flapping with coasting, a Veery flaps its wings constantly for hours as it migrates through the night sky.

The morning I saw the Veery pictured here was one of those mornings that seemed made for birding. Birds were singing all around me. It was like taking a bird shower! I watched this bird for a long time. Scarcely moving, it sat contentedly on its limb. The male and female are very similar, so I am not sure which this is.

Contentment

Being content with what we have is a godly characteristic. The contented person is happy with his meager things. He can take the few things he has and make the most out of them. There is a reason the Bible tells us to be content with the things we have. God knows that if we are content, we will always have enough. The opposite is also true—if we are not content, we will never have enough.

Be content like the Veery. It seems to be happy with the limb it has found. It was probably full from breakfast, so it found a limb where it could sing in contentment. Are you content enough to sing praises to your Creator? Can you sing even if you don't have everything you want? If you learn to be content, you'll be surprised what God can do even if you do not have everything you desire.

American Robin

The American Robin is in the thrush family. This is easy to see in young robins, as they are speckled like other thrushes. Robins have been a favorite since the first settlers came to this country. They named this bird Robin Redbreast because it reminded them of the robin of their English home. Today this thrush is known as the American Robin and lives throughout most of the United States and Canada. It is one of the most abundant birds in North America.

Swallows chatter, sparrows chirp, cardinals whistle, and bluebirds warble, but robins carol. It is usually one of the first birds you hear in the morning, and I love to hear its cheerful song.

A robin likes to eat earthworms, grubs, and berries. It has a familiar pattern as it crosses the yard in search of food. It hops forward, cocks its head, hops again, and then again, until it finds an earthworm.

The robin in the photo is a partial albino. Albinism is a loss of pigmentation in animals and birds that turns them white. Even people can have albinism. If this robin were fully albino it would be completely white with pink eyes. Isn't it pretty? The other robins do not care if it is not like them.

Kindness

If you travel around the world you will find many people who look or live different from us. Some live in big mansions, some in ordinary houses, and some in houses made of sticks and mud. Some people eat lots of rice, others eat lots of fish, and some eat lots of cheese. But really, it doesn't matter what the people look like, what kind of houses they live in, or what they eat. What matters is that we learn to love other people. God loves all people all over the world.

The next time you see a person who is a little different, think about this robin. Then treat the person like you would want to be treated. Be kind to people even if they seem a little different, and you will discover that the differences between you soon go away. A smile can often turn strangers into friends.

Brown Thrasher

The Brown Thrasher is a beautiful bird even if it is mostly brown. This gifted songster can sing more songs than any other North American bird. Its song is similar to a mockingbird, but each phrase is repeated twice instead of three times like a mockingbird.

Even though the Brown Thrasher looks like a thrush, it is not in the thrush family. Unlike a thrush, it likes to live near thickets or briar patches. I have seen many of them. Sometimes they are out foraging for food in grassy areas, and we even have a few that visit our feeder. They are alert but not easily frightened. I was surprised how close this fellow in the photo allowed me to get. Brown Thrashers generally don't like people to get too close to them.

When the Brown Thrasher is ready to build a nest, generally in May, it builds a bulky nest of small branches, thorny twigs, leaves, grasses, and plant stems. When all is finished, it lays four or five heavily speckled bluish or greenish-white eggs.

If you do find a nest, don't get too close. Brown Thrashers defend their nest aggressively and have been known to strike people hard enough to draw blood.

Worship

The Brown Thrasher almost sounds like it is talking to itself. It has a very interesting conversational type of melodious warbling. Do you ever talk to yourself? Did you know that the Bible tells us in Ephesians 5:19 to talk to ourselves? "Speaking to yourselves in psalms and hymns and spiritual songs, singing and making melody in your heart to the Lord."

This kind of speaking to ourselves is worshiping God. God knows we cannot be grumpy when we speak to ourselves in this way. Look at the words *psalms, hymns, spiritual songs, singing,* and *melody.* These are positive words and have an uplifting ring to them.

Make it a habit to worship God. Make melody in your heart to the Lord. When we worship God, a host of blessings come our way. Joy is one of those things. Going through the day in song like the Brown Thrasher is one way to express that joy.

Cedar Waxwing

The Latin name for the Cedar Waxwing means "silk tail." How fitting! No other bird looks quite as silky and elegant as the Cedar Waxwing.

These medium-sized birds love berries. They also love one another, or so it appears. They might not understand love as we do, but we know they enjoy being together. They usually travel together in flocks. Seldom will you see only one waxwing except when they are ready to nest. Then they separate into pairs and lay their five bluish or slate-colored eggs.

Where we live there is an abundance of berries. You can always depend on the Cedar Waxwings to come in large flocks as soon as the berries ripen. Day after day they come and eat until the berries are gone. A few days ago a flock of American Robins and Cedar Waxwings came into our yard, and in about a day they stripped the winterberry shrubs of their bright red berries.

The Cedar Waxwing lives throughout the United States. In the winter many of them migrate to the southern states.

Being Sociable

The Cedar Waxwing wears a black mask, has a white crest on its head, red in its wings, and yellow at the tip of its tail. It is a beautiful bird. And so is its personality. It loves others.

Being with other people helps us in many ways. I find joy in fellowshipping with other people. We learn from them and they learn from us. Have you ever seen one of those guessing jars where you try to guess how many beans or pennies it contains? We are told that if a group of people discuss the number of things in the jar, they can get closer to guessing correctly than if individuals guess on their own.

Let's learn to appreciate others' opinions. The Bible says there is safety in the counsel of others. It also tells us to esteem others higher than ourselves. So don't be afraid to receive people who are a little different into your fellowship. Learn to appreciate them. Learn to get along with them, like the Cedar Waxwing.

Phainopepla

Though the Phainopepla is smaller than the Blue Jay, it reminded me of one the first time I saw it. Maybe it was because of the crest on its head. Though it is plain in color, its name is not. Try to say, "Fay no PEP luh" and you have pronounced its name accurately. It is a western bird, living as far north as central California.

Though they eat flies and other insects, they also enjoy the desert mistletoe and other berries. Since these berries are so low in nutrients they have to eat lots of them—over 1,000 in one day. Since they have to eat so many, the berries have to pass through the digestive system quickly—in as little as twelve minutes!

In fact, mistletoe and the Phainopepla depend on each other for survival. The bird eats the berries for food, but then the seeds get passed on. This spreads the seeds and makes them more likely to germinate.

The Phainopepla drinks very little water. It gets all the moisture it needs from the mistletoe, which gets its moisture from the trees it is attached to.

A Beautiful Attitude

People spend an incredible amount of energy and money on decorating. Then, after they have it the way they want it, they look at it for a while and do it all over. Would you say the Phainopepla needs decorating to make it beautiful? I don't think so. I like it just the way it is.

It is wonderful when a young person has developed a beautiful attitude. That young person has the foundation to be a success in life. There is something good to be said about an ordinary person who doesn't care to attract attention. We are satisfied that God knows who we are. That's the greatest honor I can think of. We might be plain, but we are attractive to God.

Serve God with all your might. Whatever you do, do it for God. The Bible says that those who want to attract attention when they do something good receive no further reward. If you do good to glorify God and don't care if others notice you, then your reward is in heaven.

Yellow Warbler

The Yellow Warbler is like a five-inch beam of sunshine, a flash of gold, as it zips through the trees catching insects to eat. If you look closely, you can see some reddish brown stripes on its breast. This cheerful bird can be found throughout the United States and southern Canada. In the fall it goes south where it is nice and warm.

The male has a beautiful song that it sings over and over. It sounds like "sweet, sweet, sweet, sweeter than sweet." A birder once reported hearing a Yellow Warbler sing its song 3,240 times in one day.

Yellow Warblers are quite common and can usually be seen if we go out looking for them. They are especially numerous along rivers and streams. They are active little birds, seldom staying in one place more than a few seconds.

The Brown-headed Cowbird is the Yellow Warbler's greatest enemy, as it often lays its eggs in the Yellow Warbler's nest. The wise warbler then sometimes builds another nest on top of the eggs. If the cowbird again finds the nest and lays another egg, the warbler scurries to build yet another nest on top. It is reported that a nest with six layers has been found.

Joy

The Yellow Warbler reminds me to be joyful. *Joyfulness* is a happy word that lightens up the world. Even the very thought of joy raises joyfulness within you. Being joyful touches others, and before long everyone is joyful. Do you think the Yellow Warbler quits singing when it has to build another layer on its nest because of the cowbird?

You can spread joy by being joyful. It is our duty as Christian people to spread sunshine so others can be happy too. Watch for the bright little Yellow Warbler the next time you are taking a walk in the woods. It will remind you to be sunshine in your world.

One way you can spread joy is to smile at people. Sometimes things do not go the way we planned, but we can still be joyful. If people want to know your secret to being happy, tell them that you know Jesus and He makes you joyful.

Ovenbird

The Ovenbird's subdued colors and its habit of foraging on the ground remind one of a small thrush. In fact, it was originally called the Golden-crowned Thrush. We now know that it is actually a warbler. The popular name of Ovenbird was given because of its unusual nest, which looks like a Dutch oven with a hole in the side. It builds its nest on or near the forest floor, often beside a downed tree.

It is most commonly found in the deep woods where the understory is dense, especially with pines and hemlocks. It can be found searching for food around fallen leaves and underneath ferns and other low-growing plants. It eats seeds, worms, snails, and insects. It has a peculiar, jerky walk.

The Ovenbird's breeding range extends over much of eastern North America and up into Canada. In the fall it migrates through the night south to Florida and Central America. Studies estimate that half of all adults die each year due to the hazards of migration.

The Ovenbird has a very charming song that enhances woodland trails and beautiful summer days. The song is an increasingly loud "teacher, teacher, TEAcher, TEACHER!"

Relationship with God

Ovenbirds enjoy the forests where they raise their young. You don't often find them in swampy areas. I guess they are like me and don't enjoy getting their feet wet!

I have never seen many of these birds, but did finally find this one in Florida. It was a special treat to see this bird since it allowed me to take its picture.

There is a parable in the Bible about a man who found a treasure in a field. To get the treasure he had to buy the field. Have you discovered the treasure of Christ? Are you willing to give up your will for Christ's will?

When the Ovenbird sings "teacher, teacher, TEAcher, TEACHER!" it has no idea what it is saying. We, however, have been given understanding. If we want a relationship with God we need to cry out to Him.

Call on God to help you through life. Call on Him with as much energy as the Ovenbird puts into its song!

Chipping Sparrow

The Chipping Sparrow is one of our smallest sparrows. It is easily identified by its red crown, which is especially bright during the summer, and by its musical one-pitch trill.

Chipping Sparrows in the northern part of their range migrate to the southern states or Mexico for the winter. They communicate with a piercing call as they migrate through the night. "Chippies" that live in the southern states normally stay there all year.

This bird's daily menu is made up of seeds and insects. It eats mainly insects during the summer. During the winter, Chipping Sparrows are nonstop eating machines. Each one must consume over two pounds of seeds through the course of the winter to survive. With an average body weight of only thirteen grams, this means a Chipping Sparrow consumes about seventy times its own weight in seeds each winter.

Chipping Sparrows rarely fly up into really high trees. They like to build their nests low in trees or in shrubs. Chipping Sparrows are not as wild and easily scared as some birds and feel right at home in your backyard.

Being Spry

I like this small bird with its cheerful chip and bright crown. It is a happy little fellow that shows little fear of me. It is confident and spry. Sometimes when I walk up close to one, it keeps on picking up little tidbits of food. I like its attitude. To be spry is to be full of life—to be active, nimble, and vigorous.

To get much done, you need to be spry. One way you can be full of life is to allow God to live in you. When that happens, it changes your whole outlook in life. It will put a spring in your step and make you happy, nimble, and vigorous.

Be spry and make the best of any situation you find yourself in. If you can change a bad situation, do so. If you can't do it alone, ask someone for help. If you can't change it, wait on God. Some people have a handicap and cannot rush about. That's okay. If that is you, you can still be nimble-minded. That means you are alert and cheerful, ready to do what you can.

Henslow's Sparrow

This Henslow's Sparrow is beautiful, isn't it? When you talk about sparrows, most people immediately think about the common House Sparrow, but we actually have more than two dozen different kinds of sparrows in the United States.

The Henslow's Sparrow is difficult to find, and most people will never see one. Its choice of habitat is fields with long grass. It spends most of its time on the ground feeding on insects and seeds. I have seen them crawl through the grass like mice.

They live in isolated communities. Unfortunately, the population is decreasing due to habitat loss. We are fortunate to live close to public grasslands where I can see and hear them throughout the summer. A number of states have listed Henslow's Sparrow as endangered or threatened. It is exciting to observe these rare birds.

The Henslow's Sparrow sings almost constantly, sometimes even at night. Its song, if you can call it that, is the shortest and simplest song of any North American bird. The two-syllable chip is so fast that it sounds like a hiccup. So the next time you are out in a field and hear a bird hiccup, it just might be a Henslow's Sparrow.

Goodwill to All

Sometimes we tend to lump people into one group without thinking. We might look at the color of people's skin or what country they are from and judge them to be bad. That isn't fair. Just because the Henslow's Sparrow is in the sparrow family doesn't mean it destroys bluebird nests or messes up your property with its nasty housekeeping habits.

The Bible tells us that we ought to treat others as we would have them treat us. Let's not judge a Henslow's Sparrow to be bad because it is a sparrow. Once you know more about this sparrow, you'll like it a lot better. It's the same with people. The more you get to know them, the better you will like them.

I have met many people from all over the world, and they are not all alike. Let's show goodwill to people and become friends with them. It is amazing what we can learn from people who are different from us.

Eastern Meadowlark

The Eastern Meadowlark seems to enjoy the north. This flashy songster is one of the last of the migratory birds to leave Ohio in the fall and the earliest to come back in the spring. They migrate in loose flocks, mostly during the daytime.

A few years ago I thought these birds were becoming rare since I had not seen very many. But then I learned their song, and now I hear them often as I travel the country roads. I like to go to the edge of a field and watch them interact with each other. They don't seem as territorial as some other birds.

Meadowlarks are scarcely ever out of a song. Their sharp and shrill song is easily identified. I learned that although the song always sounds the same to me, it actually has over a hundred different patterns.

The female constructs the nest while the male sings his sweetest comforting notes to her. The nest is built in a dome shape and placed on the ground, usually in the shelter of a thick tuft of grass. The eggs, usually four in number, are marked irregularly with reddish-brown or lilac spots.

Godly Character

The meadowlark does not have the most beautiful song, but it is nevertheless pleasing and uplifting. This bird is easily identified by its perkiness.

What do people think when they think about you? Do they say you are cheerful? Or do they consider you grumpy? Being cheerful or grumpy is a decision only you can make. No one else can do it for you. Character is not determined by where you live or what culture you live in. It is who you are that matters. That is what determines what you do and how you face life.

Be like the meadowlark and hop onto something that is higher than your surroundings. Then call out with a cheerful call. I suggest that going higher is receiving Jesus as your Savior and following Him cheerfully. As you give yourself to God, He will help you grow in godly character. He will give you strength to be cheerful instead of grumpy!

Baltimore Oriole

I don't know of any bird more fascinating and welcome in my backyard than the Baltimore Oriole. With its flashy orange and black coloring, it is certainly a beautiful bird. Its song, easily imitated, sounds like, "Here, here. Come here, my dear!"

The Baltimore Oriole lives throughout most of the eastern and central United States and up into Canada. Like most of our songbirds, it goes south for the winter.

A peculiarity of this bird is that it builds a swinging nest high in a tree. Maybe the swaying back and forth helps keep the baby birds happy! The nest is so well built that it almost never falls off. The female can spend half an hour weaving a string back and forth, just like you crochet or knit a bag, before going on a search for another long piece of string or grass.

Last spring was long and cool. When it finally warmed up, many hungry Baltimore Orioles came to our feeders. We never before had so many in our backyard. It took a lot of sugar water and grape jelly to feed our hungry visitors. I guess they were hungry after traveling all the way from Central America.

Looking Forward

Some people seem to have everything. They have good looks, a great personality, the ability to make money, and many friends. I don't think the Baltimore Oriole has the ability to make money, but it definitely has the good looks! It also has a pleasant demeanor and a nice song.

You can have a pleasant demeanor as well. Someone has said that if we give the world a smile, it will smile back. But even if the world does not smile back, we can still keep smiling.

Your experience in life might be rough. Maybe you have experienced a debilitating sickness or lost a loved one. That is always tough. But I also know you can get over it. God wants us to look forward.

It is okay to grieve; God made us that way. But we should not continue grieving. There is a time to grieve and a time to rejoice. I trust that you will move forward, placing your life into the hands of God.

Red-winged Blackbird

The Red-winged Blackbird is always a pleasant bird to see and hear early in the spring. When I hear one in March, I know warm weather will soon follow. I can listen to its "ke, kong-ker-ee" singing a long time without getting tired of it. After a long winter and the arrival of spring, it sounds like it's saying, "See, I-told-you-so."

Red-winged Blackbirds are familiar birds almost everywhere in North America—from Canada down to Texas and Florida. This bird enjoys the company of others of its kind, forming a kind of a colony. Even though they live in a community, they still have their separate territories. The male uses the red patches in his wings to attract females. It is said that they sometimes hide those red patches to better sneak into another male's territory.

The Red-winged Blackbird hides its nest among slender stems of marsh grass or in fields with tall grasses. A male Red-winged Blackbird will claim a territory for its own and then try to get as many females as it can. It acts a little like Solomon in the Bible who had many wives.

Honesty

The male Red-winged blackbird has a way of hiding its red feathers so it can steal into another bird's territory unnoticed. Then it tries to steal a female. We call that sneaky, don't we? Sneaky people like to sneak things or take advantage of others. If we do that, we are not being honest.

This is not how God wants us to live. God tells us in the Bible that when we are born again and fellowship together, we are brothers and sisters. That is good. That is how it should be. We need friends so we do not become selfish. Our friends share with us what they have learned, and we share with them. That is true fellowship.

We do not all have to like the same things, but we want to be honest in how we relate to others. Honesty gives us peace. We cannot compromise common courtesy, dependability, and honesty. The Red-winged Blackbird does not know that it is wrong to steal from others, but we do.

Western Tanager

With its orange-red head, bright yellow belly, and black wings and tail, the Western Tanager is a pretty bird. As you might have guessed, it mostly lives in the western United States. But when winter gets close, it skedaddles to Central America where it is nice and warm. There they are sometimes quite numerous. On one farm in Nicaragua, observers saw up to 110 of these birds in one day.

Their primary food is insects, but sometimes they also eat fruits. Around the turn of the twentieth century, Western Tanagers were thought to pose a significant threat to commercial fruit crops, so they were treated as pests. Today it is illegal to shoot native birds, so Western Tanagers are safer than they were a century ago.

It is thought that the Western Tanager's red head is due to a chemical called rhodoxanthin, which is found in insects that have eaten certain conifer buds. This chemical gets passed along to the tanager and is incorporated into the feathers of the head.

Enjoying Nature

I was hiking in Colorado at 6,000 feet above sea level when I got my first glimpse of a Western Tanager. When I first saw it at a distance, I thought it was a warbler. I stalked it for some time and eventually got up close. What a beautiful bird!

One of the best things you can do for yourself is to enjoy nature. You don't have to climb mountains or go somewhere far away to enjoy God's creation. Just step outside and be quiet. If it is spring or early summer, you will hear birds. Many people never give birds a thought. They are there but ignored.

Learn to identify God's beautiful birds. Enjoy the green grass and the leaves blowing gently in the breeze. Look at the beautiful flowers that people generally refer to as weeds. Experts tell us that spending time outdoors in the fresh air is good for you. Of course, we knew that long before the experts! But do we do it?

So go outside and take notice. I grew up spending much time outdoors. The woods was my playground and nature my medicine. Try it.

Northern Cardinal

A very pretty and friendly bird, the Northern Cardinal loves to sit on a branch and sing. It is a common bird in the eastern half of the United States. We take it for granted that the birds we see regularly have always been here, but that's not always the case. Historically, the cardinal was more of a southern bird and didn't appear as far north as Ohio until the 1800s.

This bird doesn't mind the winter. It enjoys eating berries and seeds that it finds in forests and fields. It also appreciates the sunflower seeds you put in your bird feeders. It has a strong beak that it uses to crack seeds. An interesting thing about the cardinal is that the male bird is very polite and enjoys feeding its mate. Good for him.

Cardinals usually mate for life. The female cardinal incubates the eggs, but the male guards the nest and feeds the female now and then. A young cardinal generally does not go farther than two or three miles from where it was hatched. If the area becomes too populated, it is forced to move elsewhere.

Cheerfulness

Have you heard the cardinal's cheery call? First it calls out "cheer, cheer, cheer." Then it says "birdy, birdy, birdy." Wouldn't you like to be an encourager like the cardinal? His song is positive and joyful. I have to smile when the cardinal cheers me on.

The Bible tells us to spread good reports and be joyful. "Whatsoever things are true, whatsoever things are honest, whatsoever things are just, whatsoever things are pure, whatsoever things are lovely, whatsoever things are of good report; if there be any virtue, and if there be any praise, think on these things" (Philippians 4:8).

Even as the cardinal sings "cheer, cheer, cheer," so we should be known as cheerful people. We should count our blessings and not our misfortunes. The Bible also tells us to "admonish one another in psalms and hymns and spiritual songs, singing with grace in our hearts."[1] Let's do that.

Let the world know how blessed you are and give a cardinal cheer to everyone.

---

[1] Colossians 3:16

Rose-breasted Grosbeak

What a beautiful bird! The Rose-breasted Grosbeak is aptly named for its beautiful rose-colored breast. It has a distinctive thick, pale bill that contrasts with its solid black head. Its lovely song is similar to a robin except faster and sweeter. It is such a prolific singer that it sometimes sings while on the nest. Even the indifferent cannot help but listen to this song with admiration.

The Rose-breasted Grosbeak lives in open deciduous woods throughout much of eastern North America. Its nest is rather flimsy and so thin that the eggs can sometimes be seen from the bottom. The male helps with incubation, taking his turn for several hours each day. They sing quietly to each other as they trade places. In the fall, they migrate south, sometimes in flocks of up to fifty birds and usually at night.

I feel sorry for the people in Central and South America where this grosbeak winters. There the male is dressed in drab colors similar to the female. But when he comes back north he is wearing his rosy breast.

Living for God

I love the enchantingly beautiful song of the Rose-breasted Grosbeak. It is so mellow and sweet, so rich and powerful. I could drink it in all day! One bird guide says its song is "as if a robin has taken voice lessons." I like that.

Even if nature is not your thing and you find it hard to identify many birds, you really should go out into the woods and try to find this bird.

The Rose-breasted Grosbeak's singing is an inspiration. God wants us to praise and worship Him. He wants us to turn our hearts to Him so we will not be drawn away to the world. The Bible says that when we become friends to the world, we become God's enemy. Let's draw close to God and worship Him.

God does not expect you to sing like the Wood Thrush or the Rose-breasted Grosbeak, but He has given you your own song. Worship and praise Him. Live for Him.

"Let every thing that hath breath praise the Lord" (Psalm 150:6).

Painted Bunting

The Painted Bunting is one of the most beautiful birds you will ever see. It is a southern bird, so you will have to go to the southern states if you want to see it.

With its red apron, green and brown jacket, and blue cap, the Painted Bunting is always ready for a day's work. The female is a vibrant greenish color. Despite their flashy colors, the males like to hide in the leaves, even when they sing. It took me a long time to find one. But it was worth the hunt.

Painted Buntings migrate to Central America for the winter. As with most small birds, they migrate at night. Due to their beauty, they are sometimes trapped on their wintering grounds and sold as cage birds.

I watched some Painted Buntings at a feeder. Sometimes they would be gone for about half an hour before coming back. They would grab a few bites to eat, and then go back into the bushes again. I noted that almost without fail the female would come to the feeder first, then after a short time the male would come out of hiding and join her.

Resisting Evil

Painted Buntings are very colorful birds. They remind me of Joseph's coat of many colors. Joseph was tempted to commit a great sin. But because he loved God, he had made a commitment that he would not sin. Because of this, he was prepared when the temptation came.

That is a good lesson for us. We should pray and read the Bible so we know the difference between right and wrong. James 4:7 reads, "Submit yourselves therefore to God. Resist the devil, and he will flee from you." As we submit to God, we will increase in the knowledge of what is right and what is wrong. As we grow to love the Lord, we will also grow to hate evil. We will learn how to resist the devil. When we resist him, he will flee.

Resist when someone wants you to do something that is not right. Resist when you are tempted to dishonor your parents. Resist mocking, stealing, evil speaking, and worldly lusts. But do not resist God or obeying your parents.

Dickcissel

The Dickcissel is a grassland bird about the size of a House Sparrow. With its black bib on a yellow chest, it looks like a little meadowlark. It is named for its unusual song, which the male repeats over and over.

Dickcissels like open fields and overgrown pastures with fencerows or a few isolated trees or bushes on which the males can perch to sing. These birds can be found in the central part of the United States. They winter from southern Mexico down to South America.

On the wintering grounds, flocks of these birds sometimes number in the millions. At this time of year, they eat mostly seeds, including cultivated grain, so they are often viewed as pests. During the summertime, however, Dickcissels are welcome birds to have in your field as their food consists largely of grasshoppers and other kinds of insects.

The male is highly territorial and watches over his territory with keen eyes. He knows that if he can claim a territory with dense vegetation, he has a better chance of attracting females to his little property. The female's nest is placed on or near the ground, usually in a slight depression beside a tuft of grass.

God's Wonderful Creation

As I drove down a gravel road in Texas, I was intrigued with all the birds. Then I saw a Dickcissel. What a beauty! I had never seen many before, but here they were plentiful, talking to each other in their peculiar "dick, dick, ciss, ciss, cissel" bird language.

I am intrigued by the Dickcissel's beautiful colors. God has made so many beautiful things. Take time to observe the beauty of nature. As you do so, stop occasionally and thank the Lord for His beautiful creation. I sometimes wonder what God had in mind when He created the mountains, the rivers, and the birds.

The next time you go outside, take special notice of how beautiful everything is. Listen intently and try to count how many birds you hear. If you live where the Dickcissel lives, listen closely, and you might hear one. Look, listen, and live for Him who made everything.

Costa Rican Birding Extraordinaire

My birding experience in Costa Rica began March 4, 2008, on a Tuesday morning. A little before five o'clock, daylight crept into the little cabin where I was sleeping and woke me up. Bird songs filled the air. How could a person sleep in the middle of something like this? Even though my surroundings were strange, and the day before had been a long one, I quickly got up, grabbed my binoculars and camera, and went out into the fresh Costa Rican morning. I saw many birds I did not recognize, but there were others I was able to identify.

As I looked around, I saw several brightly colored Scarlet-rumped Tanager males darting from tree to tree, hoping for some attention from the ladies. In a tree behind the cabin, I heard Great Kiskadees calling out their name. Stealthily I crept around to the back. When I looked up into a tree a little distance away, I was stunned—a Keel-billed Toucan! The bird looked huge as it stretched out its massive, multicolored bill. The oversized bill—hued in green, orange, red, and blue—along with its yellow bib, wowed me. I was amazed to see the huge bird so close.

Scarlet -rumped Tanager

Suddenly I noticed movement off to the side of the toucan. It was a Montezuma Oropendola. The only thing I could think of as I watched the two birds was, *Wow!* Suddenly the toucan flew across a field to another tree. As I watched it, I noticed another toucan in the same tree. Parrots that I had no name for flew from tree to tree.

After my morning meeting, I joined Pablo and Eunice Yoder, Mark Yoder, and Sanford and Martha Yoder for an introduction to Costa Rican birding. Driving out of the lowlands, we headed for the cloud forest. We actually had a dual purpose for going to the cloud forest. Besides our birding plans, Pablo and Mark were doing research for a book Pablo was writing.

We drove around the Arenal Volcano, stopping where the Yoders had lived at one time. When we were getting out of the vehicle, a beautiful Yellow-throated Euphonia flew out of a bush.

Throughout the rest of the afternoon and evening, we drove steadily higher on the paved road. Finally the road got steeper and then turned to gravel. By this time it was dark. We crept along on the gravel road for many miles, stopping often to ask directions from an occasional foot traveler. At times we stopped to discuss our options. People told us there was a shortcut, but we hesitated to take it since we didn't know the condition of the road. (The next day we learned that the shortcut would have saved us a lot of time.)

Continuing through the darkness on the dusty road, we finally saw a sign for our cottage and dinner. This was indeed a very welcome sign. When we drove up to the well-lit place, we were given a hearty Costa

Great Kiskadee

Keel-billed Toucan

115

Montezuma Oropendola

Rican welcome. After the introductions were finished, we went inside and ordered our late dinner. While the meal was being prepared, they showed us our cottages. I had a roomy cottage with three half beds.

Our meal was delicious. Spanish flew around me like mosquitoes in Liberia. I ignored the whole bunch of them. Pablo told them he was doing research for a book. He found a few more leads as the trim lady fired her Spanish at him. Once in a while someone would take pity and translate a bit of the conversation for me.

After the meal and the Spanish petered out, we decided to take a night walk through the jungle. I was given a very weak light that was terribly afraid of the dark. I almost asked Mark to shine his light on mine to see if it was working!

We had a guide who spoke no English, but his Spanish filled the brisk night air. I was last in line, with nothing but cloud forest behind me. Once in a while our flashlights and their Spanish focused on some plant. When I asked why we were walking through the jungle studying plants in the dark, they just chuckled.

I was wearing Pablo's hooded sweater. It pinched me under each armpit and refused to cover me like a decent sweater should. I thought I needed the sweater when we started off, but by the time we got back to the cabin I was sweating. I had to admit, however, that the little jaunt was fun and good exercise.

The next morning at five, Pablo was calling outside my window. I went out into the morning air as quickly as I could. I was told that our goal was to see as many birds as possible. We especially wanted to see the coveted and awe-inspiring but elusive Resplendent Quetzal. When Mark had called for cottages, he was told that quetzals would often fly around the barn while one of the co-owners of the cottages milked the cows. We were now on the way to the fellow's house to go with him when he milked. He had been our guide through the jungle the evening before, and his wife had cooked our dinner.

Walking down the dusty road in the early morning was an absolutely beautiful and peaceful experience. The sounds of dozens of singing birds filled our ears as we walked along. The lady greeted us with a big smile and a hearty *"Buenos dias."* She invited us into their beautiful, modern house for coffee and some good traditional food.

After the early morning snack, we went with our host to milk the cows. Petite Blue-and-white Swallows flew happily around us as we walked down the dusty road. Vultures circled overhead, and Red-billed Pigeons flew from tree to tree. Sanford said we were only a hair away from heaven.

Since our host had told us that Resplendent Quetzals fly around the barn when he does the milking, we climbed the gentle hill behind the barn to watch. On the one side, the narrow pasture gave way to woods. We pointed our binoculars in that direction. A flock of Brown Jays soon settled into a nearby tree.

A Clay-colored Robin chirped merrily. Suddenly a Green Shrike-Vireo flew into a tree loaded with berries. Excitement surged through us as we gazed at this beautiful greenish-yellow bird. We watched it for a while until it left as suddenly as it had appeared. A beautiful Slate-throated Redstart flew in to take its share of the berries. Resembling an American Redstart, it was a fabulous sight as it twitched its tail to reveal the white feathers. By this time we were really getting warmed up for the day.

Soon a pair of Blue-gray Tanagers came in for a meal. Tropical Kingbirds flew around us and settled on fence posts, their keen eyes open for breakfast. These beautiful birds kept us busy for quite a while. An occasional Red-billed Pigeon crisscrossed the open fields. We still had not seen a Resplendent Quetzal. Finally we left the field and walked down the road where we crossed a bridge.

Blue-gray Tanager

Pablo and I went into the woods while Mark went to talk to someone farther down the road.

When Mark came back, he informed us that the neighbors had seen some quetzals yesterday. They told us to look for a certain tree with berries. We soon found quite a few of the trees, but we did not see any quetzals. Finally we decided to go eat breakfast and then come back afterwards. We felt fortunate in finding this little town. The people were very friendly and word had gone out that we were birders. It seemed the whole town was on the lookout for birds.

We were walking up the road toward breakfast when suddenly like a north wind out of nowhere several people came running. "A quetzal!" they shouted. "Follow us!" We did not need much urging.

When we came to a berry-laden tree next to a new building site, we saw two Resplendent Quetzals, a male and a female, flitting from limb to limb. The male quetzal was the most awesome bird I had ever seen. Its bright green tail must have been at least two feet long. The vivid green bird had a bright crimson breast. As we watched the quetzals for a few minutes, more village people came running to see the splendid birds. I noticed one young man in particular who was intensely interested. He took quite a few pictures.

We were awestruck by the beauty of the birds. You

Tropical Kingbird

Resplendent Quetzal. Not all of its long tail is visible.

simply cannot see a Resplendent Quetzal so close without becoming emotional. When the birds left, it was only natural to whoop and holler to quiet the adrenaline that had been pumping through our veins.

We then walked to the barn, where we piled onto the back of our host's truck and he took us back to the restaurant to eat. When we pulled into the driveway, someone shouted for us to look up. I was stunned. The sky was full of migrating Swainson's Hawks. It seemed they just kept coming. Finally the first "kettle"[1] went on past, but in the distance we watched as four more kettles circled higher and higher until they caught the right current. Each kettle probably had at least fifty to a hundred birds. When they caught the right air current they quickly drifted off into the horizon. It was an awesome sight to see so many hawks making their way north. What a beautiful appetizer for our breakfast!

After a hearty breakfast, we once again went down the road in a vehicle to where we had earlier seen the quetzals. We had been hearing Three-wattled Bellbirds all morning, with their unusual anvil-type sound reverberating through the air. Now we heard one again somewhere in front of us. We crept through the dense woods hoping to get a glimpse of it. When we came to a small creek, Pablo said he was going back to get the vehicle and park it up a little farther.

The only other time I had ever seen a Three-wattled Bellbird was in Nicaragua, where I had finally

---
[1] A group of birds circling in a warm air thermal, usually during migration.

gotten a glimpse of one high in a tree. "Lord," I prayed silently, "I really want to see this bellbird. I hope I am not selfish, Lord. You showed us the quetzals, but I really would like to see the bellbird too."

My prayer was interrupted by Pablo's shout, "Mark!"

"Right here," Mark responded.

"Come quickly! There's a bellbird right beside the road. Run!" His voice quivered.

We needed no encouragement to hurry. I hit the road running. Mark was close behind. Pablo was standing in the middle of the road, visibly excited. He motioned to me to run faster. When I got to where he was standing, he pointed to a tall tree. I could not believe my eyes. There was the bellbird out on a limb in plain sight only about thirty feet from where we had seen the quetzal. It was beautiful!

Three-wattled Bellbird

The bird sat on the limb for quite a long time. I snapped pictures as fast as I could. The bellbird seemed to be telling us to take a good look. We did. His three wattles drooped from the base of his bill, and his white head stood out in stark contrast to his body. When it finally flew off, we whooped and hollered for the second time. We were quite emotional!

After we calmed down, we walked on down the road, but it was not long until a schoolgirl came running and excitedly exclaimed, "Quetzal! Quetzal!"

We rushed after her. There, on the tree where we had seen them earlier, she pointed out a pair of Resplendent Quetzals. The male bird was gorgeous. It flitted from limb to limb. Suddenly it flew out to a limb in plain sight and sat still, allowing us to get a good look at it. We watched it for a while before it flew into the trees and vanished. We again went into our whooping and hollering mode!

All the other birds from then on were secondary. Finally it was past lunch and we knew we had to leave. We piled into the two vehicles and left the village. When we came to the bottom of the hill, Pablo stopped on the bridge and looked down over the edge. "Hey!" he said excitedly. "There are lots of birds down there!" A Summer Tanager flew in front of us. We quickly got out and sat beside the bridge. Birds flew all around us. Suddenly someone exclaimed, "Look, an Elegant Trogon!" I got only a glimpse of it before it flew off. Clay-colored Robins flew into a small tree, grabbed a few berries, and flew off. Suddenly, without warning, the trogon was back. It picked at a few berries, then came out into the open. It was a beautiful bird, but I was unable to get a very clear picture of it.

The Collared Trogon and the Elegant Trogon look almost identical. This one was at a high elevation, so it might have been a Collared Trogon. It was a stunning bird with its green feathers and deep red breast.

On the way back we saw a Blue-crowned Motmot. It rounded out our day beautifully. When we stopped at a little town, we got a glimpse of an Inca Dove. It had been a wonderful day of seeing some of the most beautiful birds in the world. It was also a great time of fellowship in enjoying nature and worshiping the Creator who designed it all.

Blue-crowned Motmot

Sources

Some of the information I gleaned for this book came from the following sources:

Blanchan, Neltje. *Birds Every Child Should Know.* Grosset and Dunlap, 1907.

Chapman, Frank M. *What Bird is That?* D. Appleton & Company, 1920.

Kirkpatrick, J. *Rapacious Birds of Ohio.* Ohio, 1859.

Miller, O. T. *The Children's Book of Birds,* H. M. Miller, 1901.

Nehrling, Henry. *Our Native Birds of Song and Beauty*, Volumes One and Two. Milwaukee, 1893 to 1896.

Pearson, Gilbert T. et al. *Birds of North Carolina*. Edwards and Broughton Printing Company, 1919.

Reed, Chester A. *Bird Guide: Water Birds, Game Birds, and Birds of Prey.* Charles K. Reed, 1910.

Reed, Chester A. *The Bird Book*. Charles K. Reed, 1914.

Ridgway, Robert. *Manual of North American Birds*. B. Lippincott Company, 1896.

Also:
Field experience
Numerous other bird books
Wikipedia

About the Author

The author prefers being outdoors. This might be eating dinner on the patio with his wife Esther while watching the birds at their feeder, or it might be out in a field or woods somewhere with his camera and binoculars.

Birding is a favorite pastime, as well as photography. The author is not satisfied with just seeing a bird; he wants a picture of it! His goal is not building a big "life list" but seeking experiences that enhance the quality of life. That means numerous things, especially a conscientious walk with God, "who gives us richly all things to enjoy."

In addition to bird watching and photography, the author also enjoys traveling, reading, and writing. He enjoys going on trips with his five sons, who also love the outdoors. A recent highlight was going with them on a western trip, where the sons went hiking at high altitudes for three days while the author walked more safely at lower altitudes.

The author lives in Holmes County, Ohio, with his wife Esther, whom he has been married to for 47 years. They have eight grown children and 35 grandchildren. He spends as much time with them as he can. You can email the author at mastcottage@gmail.com or write to him at Christian Aid Ministries, P. O. Box 360, Berlin, Ohio 44610.

About Christian Aid Ministries

Christian Aid Ministries was founded in 1981 as a nonprofit, tax-exempt 501(c)(3) organization. Its primary purpose is to provide a trustworthy and efficient channel for Amish, Mennonite, and other conservative Anabaptist groups and individuals to minister to physical and spiritual needs around the world. This is in response to the command to "... do good unto all men, especially unto them who are of the household of faith" (Galatians 6:10).

CAM supporters provide millions of pounds of food, clothing, Bibles, medicines, and other aid each year. Supporters' funds also help victims of disasters in the U.S. and abroad, put up Gospel billboards in the U.S., and provide Biblical teaching and self-help resources. CAM's main purposes for providing aid are to help and encourage God's people and bring the Gospel to a lost and dying world.

The Way to God and Peace

We live in a world contaminated by sin. Sin is anything that goes against God's holy standards. When we do not follow the guidelines that God our Creator gave us, we are guilty of sin. Sin separates us from God, the source of life.

Since the time when the first man and woman, Adam and Eve, sinned in the Garden of Eden, sin has been universal. The Bible says that we all have "sinned and come short of the glory of God" (Romans 3:23). It also says that the natural consequence for that sin is eternal death, or punishment in an eternal hell: "Then when lust hath conceived, it bringeth forth sin: and sin, when it is finished, bringeth forth death" (James 1:15).

But we do not have to suffer eternal death in hell. God provided forgiveness for our sins through the death of His only Son, Jesus Christ. Because Jesus was perfect and without sin, He could die in our place. "For God so loved the world that he gave his only begotten Son, that whosoever believeth in him should not perish, but have everlasting life" (John 3:16).

A sacrifice is something given to benefit someone else. It costs the giver greatly. Jesus was God's sacrifice. Jesus' death takes away the penalty of sin for all those who accept this sacrifice and truly repent of their sins. To repent of sins means to be truly sorry for and turn away from the things we have done that have violated God's standards (Acts 2:38; 3:19).

Jesus died, but He did not remain dead. After three days, God's Spirit miraculously raised Him to life again. God's Spirit does something similar in us. When we receive Jesus as our sacrifice and repent of our sins, our hearts are changed. We become spiritually alive! We develop new desires and attitudes (2 Corinthians 5:17). We begin to make choices that please God (1 John 3:9). If we do fail and commit sins, we can ask God for forgiveness. "If we confess our sins, he is faithful and just to forgive us our sins, and to cleanse us from all unrighteousness" (1 John 1:9).

Once our hearts have been changed, we want to continue growing spiritually. We will be happy to let Jesus be the Master of our lives and will want to become more like Him. To do this, we must meditate on God's Word and commune with God in prayer. We will testify to others of this change by being baptized and sharing the good news of God's victory over sin and death. Fellowship with a faithful group of believers will strengthen our walk with God (1 John 1:7).